HOW CAN WE TEACH INTELLIGENCE?

ROBERT J. STERNBERG

Research for Better Schools
444 North Third Street
Philadelphia, PA 19123

The work upon which this publication is based was funded in part by the Office of Educational Research and Improvement, U.S. Department of Education. The opinions expressed do not necessarily reflect the position or policy of the Department, and no official endorsement should be inferred.

Graphic Art by Peter Robinson
Word Processing by Carol Crociante

This is a product of the RBS Research and Development Project, Keith M. Kershner, Director and the National Networking Project, Barbara Z. Presseisen, Director.

TABLE OF CONTENTS

Page

Introduction 1

Components of Intelligence 5

Instrumental Enrichment 11

Philosophy for Children. 21

Chicago Mastery Learning: Reading 31

Concluding Remarks 39

References 47

Bibliography 51

Appendix 53

INTRODUCTION

For most of this century, psychologists studying intelligence were preoccupied with a single question: "How can we measure intelligence?"   In retrospect, this preoccupation turned out to be a grave mistake.   There are several reasons for this. First, their preoccupation with measuring intelligence led them to neglect the more important question, "What is intelligence?"   If intelligence tests did not improve much over the course of the years -- and the evidence suggests that they didn't (Sternberg, 1980) -- one can scarcely be surprised. Better tests of intelligence could arise only from better ideas of what intelligence is. Curiously enough, few psychologists sought better tests through better understanding.   Rather, they sought better tests through small refinements of existing technology; but this technology was limited by the inadequacies of the meager theory underlying it (Sternberg, 1977).

Second, the preoccupation with testing was based upon certain assumptions, at least one of which was seriously in error.   This assumption was that intelligence is, for the most part, a fixed and immutable characteristic of the individual. After all, if intelligence is constantly changing, or even potentially changeable, what good could the tests really be?   With scores changing all over the place, the tests' usefulness as measures that can rank order individuals in a stable way over time would be seriously challenged.

Third, and most important for concerned educators, the preoccupation with testing and the assumption that intelligence is a fixed entity led to a neglect of what some might see as a more important and productive question, "Can intelligence be trained, and if so, how?" My research suggests that this neglect was unfortunate, because intelligence can be trained. The focus of this paper is the question of "How?" But in order to address this question, consider first just what intelligence is.

It will probably come as no surprise to you that there is no unanimous agreement among psychologists as to the exact nature of intelligence. The views presented here will therefore necessarily be, in at least some degree, idiosyncratic. Nevertheless, almost everything said here is accepted, in large part, by many specialists in the field, and especially those who have set as their goal to train intelligence rather than merely to measure it (Brown, 1983; Debono, 1983; Resnick, 1976: Detterman & Sternberg, 1982).

The "componential" theory of intelligence, as presented in my research, seeks to understand intelligence in terms of the component processes that make up intelligent performance (Sternberg, 1979). First, I shall briefly describe the theory, then review three programs that train aspects of intelligence as specified by the theory, and finally conclude with some general remarks and suggestions on the adaptation on an intellectual or thinking skills training program.

COMPONENTS OF INTELLIGENCE

The view of intelligence as comprising, in part, a set of processes differs in a fundamental way from the sort of view that gave rise to IQ tests. At the turn of the century the traditional, or psychometric, view was (and for some continues to be) that intelligence comprises one or more stable, fixed entities in the head (see, e.g., Cattell, 1971; Guilford, 1967; Vernon, 1971). These entities, called factors, were alleged to give rise to the individual differences we observe both in IQ test performance and in students' performance in school. The problem with this view is that it does little to suggest how intelligence can be modified. If intelligence is some fixed, static entity, then indeed, what could we ever do to change it? But if intelligence can be broken down into a set of underlying processes and strategies for combining these processes, then it is clear what we can do to improve intelligence: We can intervene at the level of the mental processes and teach individuals what processes to use when, how to use them, and how to combine them into workable strategies for task solution.

What, exactly, are these processes? My research suggests they can be divided into three types. The first type, metacomponents, are the higher-order or executive processes that one uses to plan what one is going to do, monitor what one is doing, and

evaluate what one has done.   Deciding upon a
strategy for solving an arithmetic problem or how
one is going to organize a term paper would be
examples of metacomponents at work.   The second type
of process is the performance component.   Whereas
metacomponents decide what to do, performance
components actually do it.   So the actual steps one
uses in, say, solving an analogy or an arithmetic
problem, whether on an IQ test or everyday life,
would be examples of sets of performance components
in action.   The third type of process is the
knowledge-acquisition component.   Processes of this
kind are used in learning new material, e.g., in
learning originally how to solve an analogy or a
given type of arithmetic problem.*
    All of this may seem very abstract, so let's
take a concrete example -- an analogy.   An analogy
provides a particularly apt example because
virtually everyone who has ever studied intelligence
has found the ability to see and solve analogies to
be fundamental in intelligent performance.
According to the traditional, psychometric view, the
ability to solve an analogy would be attributed to a
static, underlying factor of intelligence.   Charles
Spearman, a famous psychometrician around the turn
of the century, called this factor 'g,' or general
intelligence.   Some years later, Louis Thurstone,
another psychometrician, called the factor
"reasoning."   The problem with such labels is that
they tell us little either about how analogies are

---

*See the Appendix for additional examples of thinking abilities
    and executive processes.

solved, or about how the ability to solve analogous problems can be trained.

In contrast, a process-based approach seeks to identify the mental processes used to solve the analogy (or the problem). So consider the processes one might use in solving an analogy, such as WASHINGTON is to ONE as LINCOLN is to (a) FIVE, (b) FIFTEEN, (c) TWENTY, (d) FIFTY. First, one must decide what processes to use, a decision that is metacomponential in nature. Next, one must decide how to sequence these processes so as to form a workable strategy for analogy solution, another metacomponential decision. Then, one must use the performance components and strategy one has selected actually to solve the problem. It appears, through experimental data we have collected, that what people do is to ENCODE as needed relevant attributes of the terms of the analogy, for example, that WASHINGTON was the first president of the United States, that he was a Revolutionary War general, and that his is the portrait that appears on a one dollar bill. Next, they INFER the relation between the first two terms of the analogy, perhaps in this case recognizing that the basis of the analogy might be either WASHINGTON as first president or WASHINGTON as the portrait on the one dollar bill. Then, they MAP the relation they have inferred in the first part of the analogy to the second part of the analogy (that is, from the WASHINGTON part to the LINCOLN part), perhaps recognizing that the topic of the analogy is some property of U.S. presidents. Next, people APPLY the relationship they inferred in the first part of the analogy, as mapped to the second part of the analogy, from the third term so as to select the best alternative. In this case, FIVE is the preferred alternative, because it enables one to carry through the relation of portraits on currency (that is, LINCOLN's portrait is on the FIVE dollar bill just as WASHINGTON's is on the ONE dollar bill). Finally, individuals will RESPOND with their selected response alternative. Although this account is a simplification of the model of reasoning by analogy I have proposed (Sternberg, 1977), it will give you an idea of the kind of theorizing that goes into a process-based account of intelligent performance.

Now, how can the metacomponents and performance components of intelligence be trained? How can one make students into better problem solvers who will be better at structuring and then solving problems than they would be on their own? I can recommend to you three widely disseminated programs of which I think highly. Each program has its unique set of strengths, and, as would be true of any program, each has weaknesses.

INSTRUMENTAL ENRICHMENT

The first training program is Reuven Feuerstein's (1980) "Instrumental Enrichment" (IE) program. This program was proposed originally for use with children showing retarded performance, but has since been recognized by Feuerstein and others to be valuable for children at all levels of the intellectual spectrum. The program is based upon Feuerstein's theory of intelligence, which emphasizes what I refer to as metacomponential and performance-componential functioning.

Feuerstein's IE program in intended to improve cognitive functioning related to the input, elaboration, and output of information by an individual. Feuerstein has compiled a long list of cognitive deficits he believes his program can help correct. This list includes, among other deficits:

- unplanned, impulsive, and unsystematic exploratory behavior

- lack of, or impaired, capacity for considering two sources of information at once, reflected in dealing with data in a piecemeal fashion rather that as a unit of organized facts

- inadequacy in experiencing the existence of an actual problem and subsequently in defining it

- lack of spontaneous comparative behavior or limitation of its appearance to a restricted field of needs

- lack of, or impaired, strategies for hypothesis testing

- lack of orientation toward the need for logical evidence

- lack of, or impaired, planning behavior

- episodic grasp of reality.

Feuerstein seeks through his IE program to correct these deficits, and at the same time, to increase the student's intrinsic motivation and feelings of personal competence and self-worth.

What are some of the main characteristics of the Feuerstein program? The materials themselves are structured as a series of units, or instruments, each of which emphasizes a particular cognitive function and its relationship to various deficiencies. Feuerstein defines an instrument as something by means of which something else is effected; hence, performance on the materials is seen as a means to an end, rather than as an end in itself. Emphasis in analyzing IE performance is on processes rather than products. A student's errors provide insights into how the student solves problems. Instrumental Enrichment does not attempt to teach either specific items of information or formal, operational, abstract thinking by means of a well-defined, structured knowledge base. To the contrary, it is as content-free as possible.

The IE program consists of 13 different types of exercises, which are repeated in cycles throughout the program. Listed here are the kinds of materials in the program, in order to convey a sense of the types of activities in which students commonly engage (Feuerstein, 1980):

- **Orientation of Dots** -- The student is presented with an amorphous two-dimensional array of dots. The student's task is to identify and outline, within this array of dots, a set of geometric figures, such as squares, triangles, diamonds, and stars. For example, the student might see at the left a picture of a square and a triangle situated to the bottom right of the square. The student would have to use the dots to draw a square with a triangle below and to the right of the square.

- **Comparisons** -- In one form of comparison exercise, the student is shown a picture at the left, say, two small apples that have no internal shading or coloring. The student is also shown two pictures at the right. In one picture, the student might see a single apple, larger than the ones at the left, and fully shaded inside. In the other picture, the student might see three apples rotated to an upside-down position that are also larger in size than the two apples at the left. The student's task is to indicate in each picture which of the attributes of direction, number, color, form, and size differ between the picture at the left and each of the pictures at the right.

- **Categorization** -- In one categorization task, the student is shown pictures of common objects and asked to name each one. After the student has done so, he or she is asked to list those names of objects that fit into each of a set of categories, such as means of transportation, clothing and footwear, objects that give light, tools, and furniture.

- **Temporal Relations** -- In one problem of this type, the student is confronted with pairs of temporal durations, such as "one year" and "eleven months." The student is asked to indicate whether the first duration is greater than, equal to, or less than the second duration.

- **Numerical Progressions** -- In one kind of numerical progression problem, the student is given the first number in a sequence and a rule by which the sequence can be continued, for example, +3, -1. The student then has to generate the continuation of the sequence.

- **Instructions** -- These tasks require a student to understand and follow instructions. For example, the student might be told that he or she should do the following: "On a line draw a triangle, two squares, and a circle, not according to size order.   The squares are to be equal size; the triangle is to be larger than the square and smaller than the circle; and the largest figure is to be on the left side."

- **Representational Stencil Design** -- In these tasks,   the student must construct mentally, not   through motor manipulation, a design that   is   identical   to   that   in   a colored standard.   Colored stencils, some of which are solid and some of which are patterned, are   printed on a poster, and the student re-creates   the given design by referring to the   standard stencils that must be used and by   specifying   the order in which they must be mentally superimposed on each other.

- **Transitive Relations** -- In this task, the student   must   recognize   relations   between nonadjacent   items   in   an underlying mental array.   For example, the student might be told   that   "Adam   likes   math more than history,   and history less than geography. Is it   possible to know which Adam likes more, math or geography?

What   are   the   strengths   and   weaknesses of Feuerstein's IE program?   Consider some of each:

- On the positive side, the IE program (a) can be used with children having a wide range in

age (from upper grades of elementary school
to early high school), ability levels (from
the retarded to the above average), and
socioeconomic groups; (b) is well liked by
children and appears to be effective in
raising their intrinsic motivation and
self-esteem; (c) is well packaged and
readily obtainable; and (d) appears
effective in raising children's scores on
ability tests. Indeed, most of the training
exercises contain items similar or identical
to those found on intelligence and multiple
aptitude tests, so that it should not be
totally surprising that intensive practice
and training on such items should raise
these test scores.

- On the more negative side: (a) The program
requires extensive teacher training, which
must be administered by a designated
training authority for the duration of the
program. (b) The isolation of the problems
from any working knowledge or discipline
base (such as social studies or reading, for
example) raises questions regarding the
transferability of the skills to academic
and real-world intellectual tasks,
especially over the long term. (c)
Despite Feuerstein's aversion to IQ tests,
the program seems to train primarily those
abilities that IQ tests tap, rather than a
broader spectrum of abilities that goes
beyond intelligence as the tests measure it.

To sum up, then, Feuerstein's Instrumental Enrichment program is an attractive package in many respects, although it has limitations with regard to breadth of skills trained and potential power for generalization. Nevertheless, it is among the best of the available programs that emphasize thinking skills training. Probably, it has been the most widely used and field-tested program, both in this country and abroad. As a result, it can be recommended for use with both members of the majority culture and members of other cultures and subcultures as well.

PHILOSOPHY FOR CHILDREN

Matthew Lipman's "Philosophy for Children" program is about as different from Reuven Feuerstein's Instrumental Enrichment program as a program could be (Lipman, Sharp, & Oscanyan, 1980) Yet, it seeks to foster many of the same intellectual skills.

Philosophy for Children consists of a series of texts in which fictional children spend a considerable portion of their time thinking about thinking, and about ways in which better thinking can be distinguished from poorer thinking. The keys to learning presented in the program are identification and simulation: Through reading the texts and engaging in classroom discussions and exercises that follow the reading, the author's objective is for students to identify with the characters and simulate for themselves the kinds of thinking depicted in the program.

Lipman has listed 30 thinking skills that Philosophy for Children is intended to foster (in children of the upper elementary school, generally grades 5-8). A representative sampling of these skills included the following:

- **Concept Development** -- In applying a concept to a specific set of cases, children should be able to identify those cases that are clearly within the boundaries and those that are clearly outside. An example the

instructional   unit utilizes to develop this
skill   is   the   concept   of   friendship.
Children are asked to consider their answers
to   questions such as whether people have to
be   of   the   same age to be friends, whether
two people can be friends and still not like
each   other   very   much,   and   whether it is
possible for   friends   ever   to   lie to one
another.

- **Generalization** -- Given a set of facts,
students should be able to note uniformities
or   regularities,   and be able to generalize
these   regularities   from given instances to
similar ones. For example, children might
be   asked   to   consider generalizations that
can be drawn from a set of given facts, such
as "I get sick when I eat raspberries; I get
sick   when   I   eat   strawberries; I get sick
when I eat blackberries."

- **Formulating Cause-Effect Relationships** --
Students   should   be   able   to   discern   and
construct   formulations   indicating
relationships   between   causes   and effects.
For   example, students might be given a
statement   such   as   "He threw the stone and
broke the window," and then be asked whether
the   statement   necessarily   implies   a
cause-effect relationship.

- **Drawing Syllogistic Inferences** -- Students
should   be   able to draw correct conclusions
from valid syllogisms, and recognize invalid

syllogisms when they are presented. For example, students might be given the premises "All dogs are animals; all collies are dogs," and be asked what valid inference they can draw from these premises.

- **Consistency and Contradiction** -- Students should be able to recognize internal consistencies and inconsistencies within a given set of statements or other data. For example, they might be asked to ponder whether it is possible to eat animals if one genuinely cares about them.

- **Identifying Underlying Assumptions** -- Students should be able to recognize the often hidden assumptions that underlie statements. For example, they might be given the following sentences: "I love your hair that way, Peg. What beauty parlor did you go to?" and be asked to identify the hidden assumption underlying the question.

- **Grasping Part-Whole Connections** -- Students should be able to recognize relationships between parts and wholes and to avoid mistakes in reasoning based upon identification of the part with the whole, or vice versa. For example, students might be asked to identify the part-whole fallacy underlying the statement, "If Mike's face has handsome features, Mike must have a handsome face."

- **Working with Analogies** -- Students should be able to form and identify analogies. For example, they should be able to solve an analogy such as GERM is to DISEASE as CAN is to (a) WAX, (b) WICK, (c) WHITE, (c LIGHT.

The skills trained through the Philosophy for Children program are conveyed through a series of stories about children. Consider, for example, the first chapter of **Harry Stottlemeiser's Discovery,** the first book in the program series. In this chapter about the consequences of Harry's falling asleep in science class, children are introduced to a wealth of thinking skills. For instance:

- **Problem Formulation** -- Harry says that "All planets revolve about the sun, but not everything that revolves about the sun is a planet." He realizes that he had been assuming that just because all planets revolve about the sun, everything that revolves about the sun must be a planet.

- **Nonreversibility of "All" Statements** -- Harry says that "A sentence can't be reversed. If you put the last part of a sentence first, it'll no longer be true." For example, he cannot convert "All model airplanes are toys" into "All toys are model airplanes."

- **Reversibility of "No" Statements** -- Lisa, a friend of Harry's realizes that logical "no" statements can be reversed. "No submarines are kangaroos," for example, can be converted to "No kangaroos are submarines."

- **Application of Principles to Real-Life Situations** -- Harry intervenes in a discussion between two adults, showing how a principle he had deduced earlier can be applied to falsify one of the adult's arguments.

Each chapter contains a number of "leading ideas." In Chapter 1 of **Harry Stottlemeier's Discovery,** for example, the leading ideas are the process of inquiry, discovery, and invention. The teacher's manual of the program provides a discussion plan and a series of exercises corresponding to each leading idea. For example, one of the exercises under the discovery and invention leading idea provides students with a number of items, such as electricity, electric light bulbs, magnetism, magnets, television, and the Pacific Ocean. Students are asked to classify each item as either a discovery or an invention, and then to justify their answer. Another exercise has students write a paragraph on a topic such as "My Greatest Discovery," or "What I'd Like to Invent."

The nature of the Philosophy for Children program may be further illustrated be comparing it to Feuerstein's program. The notable similarity between the two programs is that both seek to train thinking skills, especially those referred to earlier as executive processes (metacomponents) and nonexecutive processes (performance components). But given the basic similarity of goals, the differences between the actual programs are striking.

First, whereas Feuerstein's program minimizes the role of knowledge and customary content, Lipman's program maximizes such involvement. Although the introductory volume, **Harry Stottlemeier's Discovery,** is basically philosophical in tone, the subsequent volumes -- **Mark, Pixie, Suki,** and **Lisa** -- each emphasize infusion of thinking skills into a different content area, such as art, social studies, and science.

Second, whereas the material in Feuerstein's program is highly abstract and contains only a minimal verbal load, the material in Lipman's program is conceptually abstract but is presented through wholly verbal text that deals with highly concrete situations.

Third, there is much more emphasis on class discussion and interchange in Lipman's program than in Feuerstein's program. However, the written exercises are less important in Lipman's program.

Fourth, Feuerstein's program was originally designed for retarded learners, although it has since been extended to children all along the continuum of intellectual ability. Lipman's program seems more oriented toward children of at least average ability on a national scale of norms. Moreover, the reading in Philosophy for Children will be a problem for children much below grade level in reading skills.

What are the strengths and weaknesses of Lipman's Philosophy of Children program? Consider these:

- The program has some outstanding strengths: (a) The stories are exciting and highly motivating to upper elementary school children. (b) The program is attractively packaged and easily obtainable. (c) Tests of the program have shown it to be effective in raising the level of children's thinking skills. (d) The infusion of the thinking skills into content areas should help assure durability and at least some transferability of learning attained through the program. (e) The thinking skills taught are clearly the right ones to teach for both academic and everyday information processing. No one could possibly complain that the skills are only relevant for IQ tests, although, in fact, the skills clearly will be relevant for performance on such tests.

- The Philosophy for Children program has some limitations that ought to be considered prior to school adoption: (a) Students of below-average or even low-average intellectual capabilities may have difficulty both with the reading and the reasoning involved in the program. (b) Students from lower-class and even lower-middle-class backgrounds may have trouble relating to the characters in the stories, who come across as very middle- or even upper-middle-class in their values and orientation. (c) The success of the program will probably be at least as dependent upon

the   teacher as upon the specific materials.
This is a program that could work
outstandingly well with a highly intelligent
teacher, but fail miserably with a
mediocre or even below-average teacher who
may not be able to engender the kind of
attitude of classroom inquiry the program
needs. Indeed, some teachers may themselves
have trouble with the thinking skills taught
by the program.

In   summary,   Lipman's program for training
thinking skills is excellent, although it is limited
somewhat by the range of students for whom it would
be appropriate. There is no program of which I am
aware that is more likely than this one to teach
durable and transferable thinking skills.

CHICAGO MASTERY LEARNING:
READING

Whereas the Instrumental Enrichment and Philosophy for Children programs emphasize thinking skills (metacomponents and performance components), the Chicago program emphasizes knowledge-acquisition components (Jones, 1982). Obviously, the distinction between thinking and learning skills is a fuzzy one at best. Nevertheless, the distinction is a useful one for discerning relative emphases in these various programs.

The Chicago program, developed by Beau Fly Jones in collaboration with others, equips students with the learning skills they will need in order to succeed in school and in their everyday lives. Like Lipman's Philosophy for Children, this program is written for children roughly in grades five through eight. There are four books (tan, purple, silver, and gold), each of which teaches somewhat different skills. The emphasis in all four books, however, is on learning to learn. Within each grade (color) level, there are two kinds of units: comprehension and study skills.

Consider, for example, the purple-level sequence. The comprehension program contains units on sentence context, mood in reading and writing, complex information, comparisons, character analysis, and facts and opinions. The study skills program contains units on parts of a book, graphs and charts, preview-question-read, textbook chapter study, major and minor ideas, and parallel structure outlining.

The silver-level sequence for comprehension contains units on figurative language, word meaning from context, complex inferences, story and play analysis, story and play completion, signs, and symbols. The sequence for study skills contains units on factual support, research aids, outline form notetaking, summaries and generalizations, road maps, and forms and directions.

The Chicago program is based upon the belief that almost all students can learn what only the best students currently learn, if only they are given the appropriate learning opportunities. Achieving such a level of mastery requires systematic and frequent use of formative and diagnostic testing within each of the instructional units. Instruction is done in groups, with individual assistance and remediation added as necessary. Because students typically enter the classroom situation with differing skills and levels of proficiency in the exercise of these skills, instructional units begin with simple, concrete, literal, and familiar material, and proceed gradually to the more complex, abstract, inexplicit, and unfamiliar material.

Each instructional unit in the Chicago program contains several parts: core student activities, optional teaching activities, formative tests, and subject-related applications. Students and teachers are thus provided with a wide variety of materials from which to select and, on the basis of which, to develop the various skills taught by the program.

The number and variety of exercises in the

Chicago program is so great as to rule out the possibility of providing here a fair sample of the kinds of materials the program includes. Thus, I can make no claim that the few examples below are representative of the program as a whole:

- **Using Sentence Context** -- In one type of exercise students read a sentence containing a new word for them to learn. They are assisted in using cues in the sentence that help in decontextualization of the word's meaning. They are then asked to figure out the word's meaning.

- **Mood in Reading and Writing** -- Students are given a sentence from either an expository or fictional text. They are asked to choose which of three words (or phrases) best describes the mood conveyed by the sentence.

- **Comprehending Comparisons** -- Students are taught about different kinds of comparisons. They are then given some example comparisons and are asked to elaborate upon the meanings of these comparisons, some of which are metaphorical.

- **Facts and Opinions** -- Students are taught ways in which to distinguish facts from opinions. They are given a passage to read, along with some statements following the passage. Their task is to indicate which statements represent facts and which represent opinions.

The Chicago program is similar to the Instrumental Enrichment and Philosophy for Children programs in its direct teaching and cognitive skills. The program differs in two respects, however. First, the program resembles typical classroom curriculum more than the other two programs do. Thus, whereas implementation of either of the other two programs would usually require a policy decision to add thinking skills as an additional part of the curriculum, the Chicago program could very well be introduced in the context of the existing curriculum. The program does fit into a specific curriculum area that is common in schools, namely, reading. The Lipman program would fit into a philosophy curriculum, if any school offered such instruction. The Feuerstein program would be unlikely to fit into any existing curricular program, except those explicitly devoted to teaching thinking skills. Second, the Chicago program's emphasis, as mentioned earlier, is more on learning skills, whereas the emphasis of the other two programs tends more to be on thinking skills. Finally, the Chicago program seems most broadly applicable to a wide range of levels of student ability, including both those who are above and who are below grade level.

Like all programs, the Chicago program has both strengths and weaknesses.

- I believe its most notable strengths are: (a) the wide range of students to whom it can be administered, both in terms of intellectual levels and socio-economic backgrounds;   (b) the relatively lesser amount of teacher training required for this program's implementation; (c) the ease with which the program can be injected into existing curricula; and (d) the immediate applicability   of the skills learned to school and other life situations.   The program developer has indicated to me that students in the program have shown significant   pretest-to-posttest gains in achievement from the program. However, to my knowledge, there have been no tests of the program in controlled experiments.

• As for weaknesses, or at least limitations, compared to the IE and Lipman programs: (a) The materials appear less likely to be intrinsically motivating to students than the materials in the other two programs considered above.   (b) The skills trained by the Chicago program are within a more limited domain (reading and perhaps verbal comprehension, in general) than in some other programs. (c) The program appears not to have been fully evaluated experimentally.

In conclusion, the Chicago Mastery Learning Program offers an attractive means for teaching learning skills in the context of a reading program. The materials are carefully prepared and wide ranging, and should meet the needs of a wide variety of schools.

CONCLUDING REMARKS

Do we really need intervention programs for training students in intellectual skills? The answer is clearly "yes." During the last decade or so we have witnessed an unprecedented decline in the intellectual skills of our children (Wigdor & Garner, 1982). One can see this, of course, from the decline in scores on tests such as the Scholastic Aptitude Test (SAT), but college professors don't need SAT scores to appraise the decline: They can see it in the poorer class performance, particularly in reading and writing, of their students. Moreover, thinking skills are needed by more than the college-bound population. Perhaps intellectual skills could be better trained through existing curricula than they now are. But something in the system is not working, and I view programs such as those described here as exciting new developments for reversing the declines in intellectual performance we have witnessed in recent years.

How does one go about choosing the right program for one's particular school and student needs? I believe that wide-ranging research is needed before selecting any one of several programs for school or district-wide implementation. The program one selects will depend upon the (a) grade level of the students, (b) socio-economic level of the students, (c) intellectual level of the students, (d) particular kinds of skills one wishes to teach, (e) amount of time one can devote to training students, (f) one's philosophy of intellectual skills training (e.g., whether the training should be infused into or separated from regular curricula, and (g) one's financial resources, among other things. Clearly, the decision of which program to use should be made only after extensive deliberation and consultation, preferably with people who have expertise but not a vested interest in the implementation of one particular program or another.   Consider the possibilities of inservice or staff development in this area.   Another source of information for any district is to survey its own strengths and weaknesses in teaching thinking already.

Although I do not believe that there is any one particular training program that is optimally suited to everyone, I believe that there are some general guidelines that can be applied to selection of a program and that apply across the board to all decisions of this kind. These guidelines are the following (see also Sternberg, 1983):

- The program should be based upon a psychological theory of the intellectual processes it seeks to train, and upon an educational theory of the way in which the processes will be trained. A good pair of theories should state which processes are to be trained, how the processes work together in problem solving, and how the processes can be taught so as to achieve durability and transfer of training.   There are innumerable programs that seek to train intelligence. Most of them are worth little or nothing. One can immediately rule out large numbers of the low-value programs by investigating whether they have any theoretical basis. The three programs I have described are excellent examples of programs with both strong psychological foundations and strong educational foundations. On the one hand, it doesn't matter how good the teaching is if the program isn't teaching the right things. On the other hand, it doesn't matter how good the content of the program is if it is not taught in a way that engages and enriches students.

- The program should be socio-culturally appropriate for the students to whom it is being administered. It should be clear from the examples of programs described here that programs differ widely in terms of the student populations to whom they are targeted. The best intentions in such a program may be thwarted if the students cannot relate the program both to their cognitive structures and to the world in which they live when they leave the school. Students may be turned off by and actually rebel against programs that are socio-culturally inappropriate for them.

- The program should provide explicit training both in the mental processes used in task performance (performance components and knowledge-acquisition components) and in self-management strategies for using these components (metacomponents). Many of the early attempts at process did not work because investigators assumed that just teaching the processes necessary for task performance would result in improved performance on intellectual tasks.   The problem was that students often did not learn when to use the processes or how to implement them in tasks differing even slightly from the ones on which they had been trained.   In order to achieve durable and transferable learning, it is essential that students be taught not only to perform tasks but when to use the strategies they are taught and how to implement them in new situations.

• The program should be responsive to the motivational as well as the intellectual needs of the students.   A program that does not adequately motivate students is bound to fail, no matter how adequate or even excellent the cognitive component may be. It is not enough to have solid cognitive training: One must induce students to want to learn what is trained, and to use it, as needed.

• The program should be sensitive to individual differences. Individuals differ greatly in the knowledge and skills they bring to any educational program. A program that does not take these individual differences into account will almost inevitably fail to engage large numbers of students.

- The program should provide explicit links between the training it provides and functioning in the real world. Psychologists have found that transfer of training does not come easily. One cannot expect to gain transfer unless explicit provisions are made in the program so as to increase its likelihood of occurrence.

- Adoption of the program should take into account demonstrated empirical success in implementations similar to one's own planned implementation. Surprisingly, many programs have no solid data behind them. Others may have data that is relevant only to school or student situations quite different from one's own.

- The program should have associated with it a well-tested curriculum for teacher and student training. The best program can fail to realize its potential if teachers are insufficiently or improperly trained. The program is much more likely to succeed if it provides clear and usable teacher training, so as to guarantee that the program is implemented in an effective way.

- Expectations should be appropriate for what the program can accomplish. Teachers and administrators often set themselves up for the perception of failure by setting their expectations for the program too high, or by setting expectations that are inappropriate. Realistic expectations are essential for this kind of undertaking.

- Once completed, the program should be fully and appropriately evaluated by competent program evaluators. It is not enough to collect subjective impressions from teachers and students. In order to facilitate future decision making, a full set of formative and summative evaluations should be conducted.

To conclude, I believe that we not only can teach intelligence, but should teach it. Programs are now available that do an excellent job of improving children's intellectual skills. The vast majority of school children are not now being exposed to process training in school curricula. Indeed, the heavy content orientation of traditional school curricula would barely allow room for such training.   It is for this reason that the time has come for supplementation of standard curricula with training in intellectual skills. We can certainly continue to test intelligence, but we can provide much more of a service to children by developing their thinking skills to related intelligence.

REFERENCES

Brown, A. L. (1978). Knowing when, where, and how to remember: A problem of metacognition. In R. Glaser (Ed.), **Advances in instructional psychology** (Vol. 1). Hillsdale, NJ: Erlbaum.

Brown, J. L. (1983). On teaching thinking skills in the elementary and middle school. **Phi Delta Kappan, 64,** 709-714.

Cattell, R. B. (1971). **Abilities: Their structure, growth, and action.** Boston: Houghton-Mifflin.

DeBono, E. (1983). The direct teaching of thinking as a skill. **Phi Delta Kappan, 64,** 703-708.

Detterman, D. K., & Sternberg, R. J. (Eds.). (1982). **How and how much can intelligence be increased?** Norwood, NJ: Ablex.

Feuerstein, R. (1980). **Instrumental enrichment: An intervention program for cognitive modifiability.** Baltimore: University Park Press.

Guilford, J. P. (1967). **The nature of intelligence.** New York: McGraw-Hill.

Jones, B. F. (1982). **Chicago mastery learning: Reading** (2nd ed.). Watertown, MA: Mastery Education Corporation.

Lipman, M., Sharp, A. M., & Oscanyan, F. S. (1980). **Philosophy in the classroom** (2nd ed.). Philadelphia: Temple University Press.

Resnick, L. B. (1976). The nature of intelligence. Hillsdale, NJ: Erlbaum.

Sternberg, R. J. (1977). Intelligence, information processing, and analogical reasoning: The componential analysis of human abilities. Hillsdale, NJ: Erlbaum.

Sternberg, R. J. (1979). The nature of mental abilities. **American Psychologist, 34,** 214-230.

Sternberg, R. J. (1980). The construct validity of aptitude tests: An information processing assessment. In **Construct validity in psychological measurement.** Princeton, NJ: Educational Testing Service.

Sternberg, R. J. (1983). Criteria for intellectual skills training. **Educational Researcher, 12,** 6-12, 26.

Vernon, P. E. (1971). **The structure of human abilities.** London: Methuen.

Wigdor, A. K., & Garner, W. R. (Eds.) (1982). **Ability testing: Uses, consequences, and controversies** (2 volumes). Washington, DC: National Academy Press.

BIBLIOGRAPHY

Information-Processing Theories of Intelligence.

Sternberg, R. J. (1978). Stalking the I.Q. quark. **Psychology Today, 13,** 42-54.

Sternberg, R. J. (1981). Testing and cognitive psychology. **American Psychologist, 36,** 1181-1189.

Sternberg, R. J. (Ed.) (1982). **Handbook of human intelligence.** New York: Cambridge University Press.

APPENDIX

Principal Abilities Underlying Intelligent Behavior

- Recognizing and defining the nature of a problem

- Deciding upon the processes needed to solve a problem

- Sequencing the processes needed into an optimal strategy

- Deciding upon how to represent problem information

- Allocating mental and physical resources to the problem

- Monitoring and evaluating one's solution processing

- Responding adequately to external feedback

- Encoding stimulus elements effectively

- Inferring relations between stimulus elements

- Mapping relations between relations

- Applying old relations to new situations

- Comparing stimulus elements

- Responding effectively to novel kinds of tasks and situations

- Effectively automatizing information processing

- Adapting effectively to the environment in which one resides

- Selecting environments as needed to achieve a better fit of one's abilities and interests to the environment

- Shaping environments so as to increase one's effective utilization of one's abilities and interests

Executive Processes

- **Problem Identification** -- The student recognizes the nature of the problem confronting him or her, e.g., in a scientific context, finding a suitable problem to work on is an essential skill.

- **Process Selection** -- The individual selects a set of processes or steps that are appropriate for solving the problem as identified. For example, the student decides upon the steps needed in order to research the problem he or she has chosen to investigate scientifically.

- **Strategy Selection** -- The individual selects a way of combining the processes or steps that have been selected into a workable strategy for problem solution. For example, the student decides how to sequence the steps of the scientific experiment in a logical order.

- **Representation Selection** -- The student selects a way of representing information about the problem. For example, the student might choose to draw a diagram, make a table, etc.

- **Allocation of Resources** -- The student decides how to allocate limited resources to the solution of the given problem. For example, the student decides how much time to allocate to doing an experiment.

- **Solution Monitoring** -- The student monitors his or her progress in implementing the chosen strategy. For example, the student realizes how well his or her experimental design is working, keeping track of results as the experiment is in progress.

- **Sensitivity to Feedback** -- The student is aware of and knows how to interpret feedback regarding the adequacy of his or her chosen strategy. For example, the student is sensitive to feedback regarding the adequacy of his or her experimental design. (For an alternative list of processes, see Brown, 1978.)

Research for Better Schools (RBS),
a private, non-profit, educational
research and development firm, was
founded in 1966. Its sponsors
include many clients from the public
and private sector who support R&D
projects that meet their needs. RBS
is funded by the U.S. Department of
Education to serve as the
educational laboratory for the
Mid-Atlantic region.

Using the expertise of some 50 staff
members, RBS conducts research and
policy studies on key education
issues, develops improvement
approaches and services for schools,
provides consultant services to
state leaders, develops products for
special populations, and
participates in national networking
activities with other regional
laboratories to enhance the use of
R&D products and knowledge.

During the past 20 years, RBS has
developed extensive capabilities
which are available to all education
professionals in the form of
practical, research-based products
and services. This publication is
one of the products of RBS' R&D
work. Related training and
technical assistance services also
are available. Your interest in RBS
is appreciated and your suggestions
or requests for information always
are welcome.